TAKE THE FIRST STEP

By: Anita Osuigwe-Spencer

Copyright © 2013

By: Anita Osuigwe-Spencer

All rights reserved. No part of this book may be reproduced in any form without the expressed written permission of the publisher, except by a reviewer.

ISBN: 978-1-62407-118-8

Published By:
iWrite4orU Publishing
www.iwrite4oru.com

Cover Designed By: Byron L. Spates

Table of Contents:

ACKNOWLEDGEMENTS

I would like to thank my mother, Evelyn, whom without her guidance, love and support I would have fallen a long time ago. My children: Mark, Malcolm, Atina and Amina who keep me young at heart and always bring a glimmering glow to my space. My wonderful grandchildren: Mark III and Channing. I never thought that I could love anyone more than I love my children; you both have stolen my heart. I'm truly blessed to be on earth with you. My stepchildren who taught me to love beyond my own seeds. My Friend, Brother, Lover and Husband, Carlos, whose love, support and wonderful lessons have allowed me to just be me without any limits. Ms. Mary Doolittle, who told me years ago that I had a book in me, when I didn't even know that I had a book deep inside. Your support and friendship will forever bring me peace.

Mr. Toure Johnson, whose friendship I will cherish until the end of time. My family: Uncle Jimmy, thank you for sharing Black history with me. You started me on this journey. "Power to the people. We shall overcome." Aunt Brenda, your creativity can't be compared. Aunt Sheryl, you are my business mentor. Uncle Bruce, thank you for teaching me how to cook fancy meals. My Sister Missy (aka) Renate. Sweet and strong—I love you. My Brothers: Juan and Adrian, the time has come for us to unite. I love you both. My cousin, Lisa Hines, things will start to happen on J1 (lol). I love you for your support.

My cousins: Andrea, Monique, Delores, JoJo—This one's for us. My dear friend General Black whose wisdom and enlightenment brought me out of darkness (RIP). My Dad: Thank you. My friends and associates around the world, I thank you for the love and support. Please don't give up on your dreams, because all of you have brought out the best in me.

With Love... Until We Meet Again,

Anita Osuigwe-Spencer

Introduction

As an African American woman, my legacy here in the United States of America has been a long journey, making me strong as my consciousness reached another level. I feel my ancestors near me at all times, but at times I don't realize how close they really are and how much I lean on them for strength and wisdom. I, like many, have been everything to everyone in my family and community with no regret. With great pride, I take on the challenge of changing myself in order to change the world around me. The wisdom that has been passed on to me is a great gift to share with my family, friends, and community. In this book, I give you me. I want people to rise in love with themselves, to increase their potential and discover a new insight on life. I grew up in a fatherless home like millions of other women, but the difference is that I know that growing up this way has made me this incredible vessel that people can learn from. The reward for sharing what I have been given is far beyond anything that I could have ever imagined. My future is bright, hopeful, and amazing because the voice on the inside is louder than the voice on the outside, and for me that equals hegemony of my mind, my spirit, and my life.

CHAPTER 1

Do You See What I See?

To connect with the world as a fatherless Black woman you have to be able to look deep into your soul to move forward. Now, if you haven't been taught to even look at yourself in the mirror to see something great, how can you look within? I was always looking, seeking, and yearning for love. It wasn't that I didn't have love; my mother's love just wasn't enough. That strong male, daddy protective love that we all seek so that the circle of life feels complete is what I was missing. I didn't have that, nor did I have grandparents to give me wisdom to grow on. My mother's mother, father, and her grandparents were dead before I was born, and my dad's mother never made an effort to be a part of my life. I met her when I was 28 years old and a year or two later she passed. I don't know how that made me feel or even if it had any effect. I wasn't connected to my father's side of the family like most other women who were raised in homes with no father. My mother didn't know much about self-esteem because her mother passed when she was young. She was faced with the responsibility of raising her sister and her other siblings went to live with other family members; family members who could have cared less about her. They just wanted the material items that my grandparents left and they cleaned her out. Everything that had value was taken. The rejection that she felt was then passed down to me and disguised as low self-esteem, and by the time I was a young girl low self-esteem had weighed me down like a ton of bricks. When your self-esteem is low you are preyed upon by family members, strangers, teachers and spiritual leaders. The people who are closest to you, as well as distant acquaintances, can make you believe that you aren't wanted, and in some cases, not loved. If you get to people's core emotions and flip them upside down in order to make them believe what you see is right, deep down they will begin to feel violated. What happened to me as a result was a constant battle within for acceptance, which I eventually had to find for myself by letting my guard down with people. I learned to stop taking everything so personally. I had to open up and train myself to love myself by meditating daily, along with looking deep inside for answers. The training was conquered throughout my life and various experiences, which weren't always great. It was at times a hellhole, but as I reached the bottom of the hole, I began to think that the top wasn't too far away.

With each trial that I went through, it became easier to love myself out of the situations, by standing positive in mind, body, and spirit. I had a fighting spirit because I always leaned on the ones that came before me. As a little girl I knew that I was of African descent and that I came from greatness. Deep in the depths of my being I could feel the ancients moving within me. I just didn't know how to apply it; I was too young to even know where to begin. I began to work on me around the age of 29 or 30, and within 2 years the way I felt about myself had reached another level. It was a turbulent time for me. I was getting out of a horrible marriage with an older man. It felt like a lifetime to leave, but within 9 months of marrying him I pulled the plug. I just couldn't breathe. A book that I needed, The Value in the Valley: A Black Woman's Guide Through Life's Dilemmas by Iyanla Vanzant, came my way. I realized that whatever you need, the universe will provide it, even if you stumble across it... and I needed a way out of my very broken marriage. I woke up one morning and I didn't know where I was for about two minutes. I was really lost, hurting and scared because I knew that I had to leave this marriage, and fast while I still had my mind. As long as you are in the right mental state you can put your life back together again.

I began planning my new life the moment I woke with love... love for myself, love for my children, and love for life. I had emotionally moved out that day, and a month later God physically moved me across town in a tiny but safe apartment where I enjoyed showers of peace. I began to like sunflowers. Bright colors danced around my new home. I could listen to music and light candles. Joy began to fill my life like never before. I shaved my hair, feeling completely free of old patterns, and locs began to flow out of my head like artwork. Was it really true? Was the old Anita dead? The old Anita would run from anything new, that way I could put people and situations in my way that weren't productive, and I could blame them for not progressing and remain in a state of anger. I almost didn't recognize myself. Was it love? It felt strange to love me. I always looked for love from every direction. Still my days of turning on myself were not over. There are times when I gave my all to realize that I just turned on myself by dealing with the same type of people that I had attracted before. It seemed like I was in waist high and sinking like quicksand. These are the times where you get out, but it happens at a very slow pace because there is a lesson to learn. Many times I found myself in the same situations over and over again and wondering

WHY? It was revealed to me by a dear friend that WHY = SELF. You have to look at yourself for the answers involving you. You simply outgrow people, family, friends, and even enemies, like you outgrew your favorite jeans in high school. I never looked at myself to see what parts I had played in the production. I just wanted so badly for things to work in every relationship, including male friends and girlfriends. In the beginning, with most things, it looks nice. However, as things become old, true colors come out and our paths begin to take different routes. As I grew, I realized that everyone can't go to the next level with you. Releasing the old and ushering in the new was a great feeling. A part of me felt sorrow because I couldn't bring everyone, but they just didn't fit on the journey any longer. Allow your goodness, grace, and assurance to take you to places that you wanted to go as a child. The child that lives in us gives us the intellectual capacity of rebirth again and again.

"FOLLOW YOUR HEART, NOT YOUR MIND. THE MIND IS THE PAST AND THE HEART IS THE FUTURE" – OSHO

CHAPTER 2

How Was I Supposed to Know?

If you know anything about trust, you know it AIN'T easy. When you're trusting you are putting belief in the honesty, reliability, and care of another. When I was 17 years old, the test came the day that my boyfriend told me that he had VD (venereal disease), not to let me know that I had it, but that he cheated on me. I was crushed from head to toe. I believed in him; I hung on his every word and now, what was I supposed to do? He was the first man that really seemed to like me and show me attention in a boyfriend kind of way. I ran in my mind, but my feet stayed planted in place looking, staring, and trying to figure out if I would trust this deeply again. Well, the answer was yes. Eventually after some serious falls, I began to trust myself. That's what I had to bring to the table in every relationship if I wanted to receive trust and honesty in return. I fell backwards and forward to really get this lesson. I had been lied to by many, but I just figured not the one I had given my heart, mind, body and soul to. I had made up in my mind that trust was for suckers, until I met up with my true self and knew that if I allowed this situation to shape my future that I was destined to run into hurt, dishonest people like me. I was long grown before the lesson hit me, and I ran into guys and girls that tested this theory often. When I let people in and I lied about who I was or what I really wanted, I got the same in return. There were times that I really thought I knew who I was. I had no idea and that again was what I got in return. I didn't begin to trust myself until I had to pick my heart up thousands of times and put it back together again because of shattering heartbreak from previous relationships. When you begin to question everything around you in silence and meditation, trust will speak loud and clear. We can choose to hang on to heartbreak our entire lives, or we can release and trust in ourselves. Trusting in yourself means trusting in your godlike self. So many times we trust in God and not in ourselves, which means we are not being obedient to the universe. We are blocking the things and people that are created for us. Opening your heart and trusting is a way to give back to the universe all that you are grateful for. You will know that you are trusting when you can feel everyone coming into your space. If you're trusting in yourself, you will be able to move quickly to keep the good and remove the not so good. When dishonest people or circumstances come into your space, their dishonesty doesn't belong to you. Now is the time that you have a choice to keep or remove. If you keep the dishonesty, this is the time to reflect on you, yourself and your trusting of self. We can and will turn on ourselves when we want to avoid making a decision of letting someone or something go, such as a bad marriage, hanging with the wrong people or a dead-end job. One wrong decision to change our thoughts and to not completely trust in our own judgment will begin to make us question all things that are to come. Meditate and pray on the situations that make you question who you are. Doubt is a good thing, a good starting point because you are not pre-judging anything; you are simply in the middle. If you go in dishonest you have already judged your future. Furthermore, with dishonesty comes negativity which will drain all life out of you in time. Offer yourself a chance to grow and become an empowered being through trusting. We often don't make moves, go for that new position, or start our own businesses because we feel that we are not worthy. It's not that you are not worthy, you just don't trust the real you inside to be who you are. Most people prey on others because people see the weakness on your shoulder. They have pre-judged you and you let them. When you allow others to trust for you, your life begins to take unrecognized turns for the worse. Trusting yourself is empowering. It gives you the balance that brings you high energy, a glowing soul and a refined mental state. It's not about who you trust; it's about trusting the GOD in you. Are you ready for Love, Inner Harmony, Outer Peace, and Happiness? Then, you have to be ready for trust because you will get all that and then some when you began to trust you.

"ONCE YOU BECOME REAL, YOU CAN'T BE UNREAL." – OSHO

Daily Steps Forward Movement

CHAPTER 3

The Fight Is On

Was I angry? Yes, I was and I thought that I had a right to be. I mean I grew up without a father and we were dirt poor. Rats and roaches seemed to be better off than I was. I didn't have the best clothes. I didn't take school pictures after the 6th grade because that's when you had to preorder and prepay. We didn't have lights most of the time so I would have to hurry home to do homework before it got dark, and the list goes on and on. When I was about 15 years old, I stopped making the list over and over in my head and realized I'm still here through it all, and in my right frame of mind. What could I do with this chance? Life wasn't over for me. I could still do some good or I could pass this rash of anger to my children and the cycle could continue. I was frozen for years trying to figure out this anger and the root of it. Did I have to be angry? That's what it means to be a strong Black woman right? To be able to stand on my soap box, cussing, yelling, and rolling my neck and putting people in their place. We have to be the leader in our homes, community, and on jobs, because our men have disappeared in one way or another.

It has put African-American women in what I call the "Angry Black Women Syndrome" state. That's what they showed us on TV and in the environment all around us in the Black community, so that is what we know. When I was growing up it was nothing to hear about someone getting beat with an extension cord, three switches braided together, or the buckle end of the belt. Was that anger passed down from slavery? Most mothers and fathers did and still do look at their children as possessions because we were once possessed on plantations and that behavior is within us at the deepest core of our being. I was on a journey to learn how to control my anger and put it in its proper place. I knew that it was OK to get angry, but not to be enraged. Were most of us in the Black community suffering from Post-Traumatic Slave Syndrome? All of these questions offered very few answers to correct some of the pain that I/we have suffered through. I wanted to be a calm, cool and collected person with my anger tucked away, but I just didn't know how. I began to read about anger and the different ways to control it, but I still didn't know the root of where it originated. I conducted research in different books and videos, and even spoke with a therapist. If we have nursed the milk of fear down through our foremothers, was anger passed down as well?

I realized in my 30s that putting to rest most of my anger was easy with a shift in my thoughts and emotions. One of my first shifts was to not take anything personal, and with that a lot of the anger situations began to disappear. When I was younger, if you talked bad about my mother or my father I wanted to fight. It only bothered me because I thought that those things were somehow true deep down inside. Things like "your mother is poor", your mother is fat", and a variety of other insults, along with the fact that I was trying to protect my father who wasn't even there to protect me. My life began to change as my four children started to get older. They were nine, six, three, and two years old at this time. However, my self-esteem was still low. Kids don't always do what you say, but they do what you do, and I didn't want angry, low-esteem children ready to click at the sound of a bell. I wanted mentally stable children who knew when to pick and choose their battles. As I studied more, I learned about the passive and aggressive anger and figured out where some of the anger came from, as well as what I could do with it. I was no longer concerned about the root. I wanted to discover how to rid myself of it. I could go on digging forever, but we all have anger deep inside. How I dealt with it was another issue, and I was on my road to recovery. I even changed my attitude and the people around me. Angry people will bring on angry situations. It's like any addiction; you recover in solitude or with the proper help. For me, anger was like a drug. I needed to cuss or tell somebody off on a weekly basis, though I would feel rotten later. In Corporate America, they train you to be angry in most positions, especially collections, sales and other high-stress jobs. They know they have to train you because it's the average person's nature to be kind and loving. Most jobs are fairly simple, but to become angry takes special training. Imagine if you worked in collections for 25 years what your health and life would be like. That's why jobs like that have a very high turnover rate. People cannot stay because the suffering is too acute. Most people that look angry are not. Their angry facial expressions are just a protective device to help them get through life. You will see some people as they age and their foreheads are wrinkled from the frowns of anger. We can't get those smiles back; we must put our anger to rest. Each moment that we stay locked away in our angry prison (which we have created for ourselves) takes years off of our healthy lives. When we allow people to push our buttons we are giving them all of the power. Our power belongs to us to do positive uplifting things with it. The people who are in our lives study us unconsciously. Some take your power from you when you need it the most. Carry your anger in a place where few are exposed to it so that the moment you want to unleash your raft you can pull it back in when needed. If they never see you getting angry they don't know what button to push, so their effort to push goes away. Getting angry doesn't work as well as it did when you were younger. The effort is far too great today. You have to exhaust a lot of energy to push anger. Time began to show me that what I focused on is what I brought on. Change your friends, family (yes, you can change the way you interact with family), job, and even at times you will have to change your home to get your anger in order. The end results are bliss, wonder, delight, wisdom and a healthy physical body.

"PEOPLE DON'T NEED YOU TO DIE TO SUFFER. THEY JUST NEED YOU TO BE ANGRY OR IN A NEGATIVE STATE OF MIND AND THEY HAVE YOU RIGHT WHERE THEY WANT YOU."—TOURE JOHNSON

CHAPTER 4

Releasing Bad Habits

Yes, I have habits. Some good, some not so good, and some just damn crazy. We have all been there, just doing things unconsciously without even blinking an eye. I have had some habits where I lost great people because I simply didn't know how to keep my mouth shut. Habits are those things that some of you wish you could shake and others of you don't even know that you have them. For example, I always felt like I had to take care of those around me. I worried about my mom with my sisters and brothers because things were always financially tight for my mother as a single parent. Sometimes to the degree of exhaustion, from running people to the store, doctor's appointments, school, cleaning and cooking and starting over again the next day, with little room for my own life and family. I knew that I was needed and it felt good, but I was doing all of those things just to capture a feeling that made me feel full, not because I wanted to do those things. I felt that if I worked hard for people, I would always have people around me, and I definitely wanted people around me so that I wouldn't have to be alone with myself.

At that point I would have to take responsibility for things in my life that I wasn't ready to deal with. I knew that if I continued at this pace I would wear myself down and have to be put in the hospital. That's exactly what happened while traveling to Atlanta one year. I was relaxing at a friend's house and my chest suddenly started hurting. I was having a heart attack and couldn't breathe, so they rushed me to the hospital. With no insurance and no money, I was treated quickly and released even quicker. That was a lesson I will never forget. I had run myself into exhaustion. It was time to STOP. Stop all of the habits that got me to this point in my life. I needed to just chill. My favorite saying is "you can't see your reflection in running water; the water has to be still." Since our body is made of mostly water I needed to be STILL and LISTEN to the small still voice inside for further instructions. You see, releasing old patterns requires that you listen to everything around you, even the things that you cannot hear with the naked ear. Your body was created in perfect harmony and it can heal itself and will tell you what it needs at all times. Habits are things that keep us in a box that is so tight it can squeeze the life out of you. After my hospital visit I began to look at old patterns and thought of ways that I could grow and release.

All of the people that once counted on me had to GO! The bad diet had to GO! In my mind I was thinking of what else I could throw out of the window. Negative thoughts had to GO! Saving all of that old stuff that was just collecting dust as reminders of the past that I cherished had to GO! I began to listen to what my heart wanted me to do, and the answers came so quickly and quietly that I almost missed some of them. As I started changing old patterns and habits, people and things began to vanish without a trace. It was like I didn't even know some of them. The ones that did stay tried a few more times to see if I still needed to be needed. They quickly got their answer. I was clearing not just my life but my mind as well. The future seemed brighter. Even the sun was vivid, and the moon became clear. I began to meditate and pray in a new way and surrounded myself with me. I would step outside of myself to observe and see the progress and watch for old patterns trying to rear their ugly head again. My life felt lighter. I began to lose weight and became more productive. Shedding old patterns isn't easy. It took years to release the smaller ones because they were tucked away so deep that I really needed to go search for them. The big habits were right there in my face so I could attack them head on, but you will find that those small habits are the ones that will get you. Samples of small habits are gossiping, looking down on people, talking with food in your mouth (well that could be big depending on your mouth), judging, half doing things, and the list goes on. Listening to your body with your heart is nurturing. When you begin to listen you can begin the healing process and releasing bad habits will become second nature. Start with what you know, like smoking, drinking, cussing, poor eating choices, driving fast, getting to work late, jealously, talking loudly, complaining about everything, and not taking any action to correct anything around you. Make a list of things that you know you can begin to change right away (it's like peeling back an onion), and start putting them in the garbage. Some of the habits and old patterns may take time and some you may need professional help with, but it is possible today to stop something that you feel that you have control over. You may feel that you are on autopilot and that God is in total control, but you do have control of the habits and the patterns that you have brought into your life. Simply put, GET RID OF THEM STARTING NOW!

"IF YOU KNOW BETTER, YOU HAVE TO DO BETTER"—ANONYMOUS

CHAPTER 5

Creating the New ME

How do you make or form anything? With time and a lot of patience. I watched myself grow up. People always say I watched this one grow up, I watched that one grow up, but we never seem to include ourselves in the watching process. Once I discovered that I could watch myself, things became much easier. I could step outside of myself and make corrections. I know at first it sounds crazy, but it's true. You can monitor yourself with ease by listening and processing your daily activities with the right breathing techniques. Here's how you know that it can be done by everyone. Have you ever had a fight, did something silly, or cussed someone out and looked back and said that was just dumb? You saw yourself at that moment, but with a delayed glimpse. If you learn the watching and observing techniques you can prevent a lot of fights, cussing and silly moves that could change or save your life. When you step outside of yourself and in those positions what happens is you can see it before it starts to develop and you can then walk away, cool down, and just think. Stepping outside of yourself can save you a kismet of heartache and pain. Creating, molding, and shaping are art forms that very few have mastered. What I do know is that everyone can't be an artist. It takes years of training and experience in any field that you are in, so creating a new you will take training and experience, such as reading new material, traveling, exploring new cultures, and research on ways that can and will make you a better person. When you are in the creation process, it can be difficult if you are not ready for the big changes that are taking place right before your eyes. The process is too much for people. Most people like their old patterns because it was much easier for them to be rude, angry, and most of all ignorant. Waking up is always so hard to do. Some can get up with ease, others need an alarm clock, and many just oversleep and miss the boat. How you want to live your life will depend on one thing—YOU. In order to create a new you, you need to start raw. It's like gathering materials to paint. Some will need God, others with need music or a book, and some will need a teacher or trainer to guide them. Supporting yourself can be difficult at times, but your environment is going to be an important start. Start by going through and cleaning your house, room, car, etc., so that you can create a thinking environment where you are clear with your thoughts. If you are looking around right now and things are a mess, usually so is your mind. Burn some scented candles or incense, dim your lights and just sit for a moment to take in the newness of the clean house, room, or car. It feels nice now that you can THINK! Thinking is a liberating experience, especially when you can see the floor. Have you ever visited someone's house and it's in total chaos and their life is the same way? You may have also visited someone's home and it's in order, which means their life is pretty much on track. Then, there are those whose downstairs is well organized and the upstairs is total chaos. These are the types of patterns that I am talking about. The old saying is "cleanliness is next to Godliness", so when you have these people who are screaming about how godly they are and their house is a mess, look out! Moving into order is taking you closer to the Divine. You are in a new position to think and be thankful for all the things that you currently have. Working on you takes time and there will be some difficult steps, but in the long run it is so worth it. The joy that life is going to bring forth can't be imagined. The people that you are going to meet, places that you are going to go by creating a new you will even surprise you. Everything starts with the core you. Life is abundant and waiting for you to grab on and ride.

Don't be afraid to take advantage of all that you have coming to you. The world is waiting.

"CHANGING MY THOUGHTS MAKES ME FEEL GOOD. I AM LEARNING TO CHOOSE TO MAKE TODAY A PLEASURE TO EXPERIENCE. ALL IS WELL IN MY WORLD"—LOUISE L. HAY

Daily Steps Forward Movement

CHAPTER 6

What You Don't Know Could Hurt You

Men, Men, Men! I had so many problems with men. There were days that I felt that this man is driving me crazy, and yet I wanted this man all around me. I was confused because there wasn't a man in my house as an example for me to see. My uncles were cool, but they weren't there daily and they had their own dysfunctions. I knew that if I wanted respect that I had to give respect. That, I was sure of. Was I supposed to do all of the cooking, cleaning, and raising of the kids? Where did the man fit in? What was his role in the house? I had so many questions with very few answers. I could watch a few shows that showcased African American families like "Good Times" and "The Cosby Show", but one was at one end of the spectrum and the other wasn't quite how I grew up. I think I fell somewhere in the middle, but that was just TV. This was real life. Getting a man was never my issue; it was keeping me and him happy at the same time. I wanted my dad in most of the men for protection and security, which for me was a big mistake. You know how you hear some women call men "daddy" or "big daddy", I think subconsciously deep inside that was another way of getting daddy love. I was on the hunt for daddy love. I even made some men into my dad by allowing them to control my everyday actions, like what I wore and who my friends were. I found myself trapped in a lot of relationships where I was being controlled and couldn't be myself because I was someone's little big girl that they were sleeping with. I would go out of my way to seek attention that I felt a man should give his daughter, such as crying a lot, throwing tantrums, and just trying to get my way. I learned that if you conduct yourself like a child you will definitely get treated like one. These immature acts left me alone fast because no one wants a child on their hands and I didn't want to be controlled. I just wanted my DAD. Once I got in my 30s I realized that my daddy wasn't coming and I needed to just grow up and fill in that void or hole with a lot of self-love. I did this by reading, studying, praying and meditating. The quality of men I dated started to change a little, only because I was changing a little. I wanted BIG love, a love you could feel across 50 states. I was willing to do the work, but I was also a mother so I had to not just find someone that suited me, but now my children were involved. I was male bashing along the way (not in front of the children), not realizing that men weren't the enemy. I was my own worst enemy for not giving me what I needed—LOVE—and a whole lot of it. Men are just as lonely as we are, and in need of love too. We have to remember that some of their fathers left also. I believe that men need a love that's almost like a rite of passage to adulthood, something to grow on; while most women need a protective, secure love. African-American men are in a unique position here in America and many places around the world. They have never been in a position to protect their families fully, the way they could before we were brought over during the middle passage. Women would be on those ships crying out for their God and men to no avail. Once we landed here, the protection was completely gone because the land and slave owners were protected by laws where black people had no rights. A woman was forbidden to marry most of the time. Their main role was to make babies for the plantation owner for profit, along with being the bed winch/warmer of the master, his brother and their sons. If the plantation owner wanted to kick the door in and take a woman out of her bed to rape, sell, or violate her at any time, it was OK because she was his property, as well as the man. These plantation owners were protected by law. Times have changed, but not that much. Instead of them knocking down the door taking the women, they are taking our men to prison in record numbers. These prisons are just slave plantations with another name. The women are left to still work for the same people that have oppressed African Americans for over 500 years. Yet, we look at men and wonder why they don't take care of their kids and women. Research has shown that some of the plantations didn't have cotton, tobacco, or corn. They would simply breed Black people like horses. On some plantations, once a woman had 25 babies she could get her freedom, and we all know that freedom is more precious than LOVE. There were people like Harriett Tubman who loved her husband dearly, but when it was time to escape he didn't want his freedom. His wife not only wanted her freedom, but freedom for hundreds of others as well. The love didn't keep her on that plantation. Someone can love you your whole life, but if they keep you in a dungeon where is the freedom? For men, there would be some plantations with two or three women and one male, and they would produce 300 slaves. It sounds impossible, but it's documented in the book *Bull Whip Days*. The male didn't have to feed, clothe, or care for the child in any way; he was just a stud on the plantation. Slavery wasn't that long ago, and some of the trauma we suffer through today is connected to Post Traumatic Slave Syndrome. If you have 25 babies and they all get sold off, or if one is sold off, there is a disconnect there, and we pass that on to the next generation.

My mother told me that her parents never told her that they loved her—Disconnect! Some children never got hugs—Disconnect! We have to understand why our community functions the way that it does. We were never supposed to marry or have families; we were a labor force for white America. To know that at any time our families could be taken from us was the most inhuman thing you can do to a group of people. The healing of our nation will begin with the women; we are choosing the men in our life without knowing their legacy, and understanding that African-American men are not our enemy. People never want to talk about slavery and the effects that it has had on us. We have been taught for years that the slavery that was put on African Americans here in America was something to be ashamed of. We must move closer to slavery, not away, so that we will know what has happened to us, our men, and our children. Releasing our fears, anger, and guilt is the most powerful thing that we can do. Healing begins deep at the core of who we are, by reading, studying, and gaining new knowledge of self with help. Not digging, staying mentally in a place of unawareness will keep you in a state of ignorance for a lifetime. Now is the time to hold your head up high and move backwards toward our powerful past to gain awareness so that you can change you and the future of the world. I'm not telling you to stay there, but visit to increase knowledge of self.

"I FREED THOUSANDS OF SLAVES, AND COULD HAVE FREED THOUSANDS MORE, IF THEY HAD KNOWN THEY WERE SLAVES."—HARRIET TUBMAN

CHAPTER 7

What Do I Do with What I Know Now?

I'm looking at life dead in the face. It was raw and uncut. I had four children at this point. No formal education, but I was smart as hell. Show me something once and I would get it. I studied the things that I needed and dismissed the things that I didn't. I was what some would call self-taught.

I knew that school wasn't for me. I didn't like the books, films, or the structure; everything was European based. I needed to do something and I was going from one dead-end job to the next. I always knew that it was something bigger for me, but what? I worked my ass off and did everything from cashiering to working in the music industry, but nothing ever stuck. I think that I was emotionally drained, and tired of working and making money for others. I was good at my jobs, at least I thought so. I got fired a few times and some I just quit. I knew that I never wanted to retire from any company, which meant spending 25 plus years working for someone else making their company a hundred times what they paid me. That was never my plan. Even as a child working for others wasn't my style. My mom was a beautician and so was her mom, but I didn't want to do that, not with all the chemicals. NO WAY! So, I started several businesses and each one tumbled. Not because they weren't good ideas, but I had no working capital to keep them going. I was 14 years old and had very little direction with business, but I knew what I wanted and that was to be self-employed. I wanted my own money to pass on to the next generation. Searching for yourself and trying to become self-employed can be very difficult for a young woman with little formal education and lots of skills, but I was determined to achieve my dreams and goals. Making a move to Jacksonville, Florida, was a last minute decision, but it turned out to be the best thing that could have happened. The future looked bright and I could get a fresh start in the South.

I had several men in my life who felt that working for others was what we were supposed to do, but deep, way deep down in my soul, I knew better. I eventually met my husband when I was about 35 and ready for something new. In walked Carlos, this beautiful, exciting, supportive and passionate brother who was open to be loved and I was ready to give him all that I had. When I first saw him I knew that I was going to love him. I could feel it.

My husband was put in my life for me to go forward, but if I wasn't ready I would have missed the lesson again. Finally, the support that I needed had arrived. I could fly, and that's what I've been doing ever since. The money didn't have to be there immediately. I realized that by saying it's not about the money I was blocking any money that was supposed to come my way, but just the belief that I could and would do it was enough drive for me. I had finally reached the point where I was approving of myself. I was fighting not to go back to self-pity and being controlled with low self-esteem; that took years for me to understand. Now I know that the possibilities were endless and that has made all the difference in the world. My husband wouldn't be able to support or love me if I didn't first love and support myself, and because of past relationships I had seen how many times that I turned on myself in the name of love. I attracted this new type of love because that's what I was ready for. All of my prior relationships prepared me for this moment. I learned some valuable lessons from all of them, good and bad. The universe knows what you can handle and what you can't at different times in your life. The things that I deal with today, I probably couldn't handle a few months or even years ago. You grow stronger daily when you change your awareness.

At this moment in time, I began to release and shed some of the old habits that I had stored away at the core of me because of this new support and love that I was surrounded by. I have no limits with the gifts that I have been given. I knew something was different because I could feel that my breathing had a more rhythmic beat to it and my headaches from stress went away. The freedom that I felt was like no other time in my life. I was at my strongest mentally and my studying had paid off. I now owned my own salon/day spa, along with a life coaching business that's going in many positive directions, and it looked like both businesses were heading for great things. The money was not all there, but at least this time I had a blueprint from my previous adventures to take a little and learn how to make it a lot, while believing that I could do it. With all the reading, studying, and the many jobs that I had, I think this time I had a fighting chance. All of those experiences prepared me for this moment right now. I am a firm believer that if you work on any job you better look, watch and take away some skills that are going to make your life at some point work for you. I was the spook that sat by the door. I know people who retire, get fired, or quit a job and have no clue what they should do next because of programming.

What did you do at your last job? How can you expand on that and make money for yourself? What systems did you learn that can improve your business or your life? This is the only life that you get. There are no do overs. What are you going to do? What are you going to come back from? Feel good about the decisions that you make. Confidence makes you feel empowered and gives you the strength to carry on in the face of adversity. Today is the day that you take a chance and give yourself a new lease on life. Releasing the negative and replacing it with the positive will shave years off of your life. Thank God for your healing daily and you will begin to feel better instantly. Tithe 10% of your time to empowering you with new thought patterns and surrounding yourself with good people that you can feel in your soul.

The people in your circle are your future; look closely at them because they are you in some way. The things that you don't like about your circle of friends and acquaintances are the things that you need to work on within yourself, so that you can move on with your life and let them go. This is where the real releasing begins.

"THE PEOPLE THAT YOU HAVE AROUND YOU SHOULD EITHER BE ABLE TO TEACH YOU OR YOU SHOULD BE LEARNING FROM THEM, BUT TO HAVE THEM AS YOUR EQUAL SERVES YOU NO PURPOSE."—ZEN

CHAPTER 8

Are You Looking in the Right Place?

What is it that we want and need from the people around us? Support. Support can be virtuous or it can be ruthless. We look to others for support and rarely do we look at our inner self. We have never been taught about loving and supporting ourselves through all situations, because most times we are either overparented or underparented, with no equal balance. Society has programmed us to become dependent on others to validate our ideas, spirit, soul, picking our mate, naming our children, what God to serve, even what to eat. We must learn to listen from that deep place in the core of our soul for the support that we need. The problems that we face are resolved in the core of our soul. The break happens when people are afraid to be still and accept the answers that flow to them ever so easily. When the answers come too easy, people become afraid that it happened too quickly. So the fight begins, not with others, but with ourselves. Some fight for years with the answers, and the support is right in front of them. People turn to drugs, alcohol, and religion for the answers that are already there, and most of those entities are just going to confuse you more than when you started with the problem. We are so afraid of the godlike qualities that are in us. How can someone make us in their image, but not install some of their qualities within us? That's like making a child and he or she doesn't have any of the qualities of the parents. The parents would then start to question whose child it is. We have moved so far from nature that we have lost the ability to support ourselves emotionally. If we can't support ourselves, we can't properly support our children or husbands. One of the reasons that the natural order of our homes are not in balance is that women today don't know if they want to be a wife or a mother first. Being a mother is a very important job. For most women, motherhood is built-in, and for others training is needed. To be someone's wife takes a different type of courage. The courage to live, sleep, work, travel, build, dream, grow, share, trust, co-parent, care for, and to love with honor and dignity. That is something that doesn't come naturally, but is either learned or taught behavior. With the right love, self-esteem, and self-support, we can begin to bring order to our homes and life. Being a wife is the first order of the house. As a woman, being a mother is a natural process; some are better at it than others, depending on what environment that you have been brought up in.

Your parenting skills are directly from your mother, or if she wasn't there then your skills are acquired from the next caregiver that was in line. We begin to connect with our children as they grow inside our body. We have a nine month jump on all of those that will love them once they are here. How we care for and support our baby before birth will determine, for some, the rest of their life. Those women going through stress and depression during pregnancy will have a child with those same disorders. A wife is an important duty to the universe that ultimately shapes the world. The house is only as strong as the woman that dwells there. If the house is weak, it is a reflection of the woman. It's a hard pill to swallow I know, but it's true. I always use the Obamas as an example. Do you think that President Obama could be the President of the United States with a weak wife? I'll answer it for you—NO! It's a lot of responsibility for some to carry, that's why we have a new generation that has no idea what's going on around them. The mothers are no longer going through any type of rites of passage. They have nothing to show them how to be a good wife or partner, so they jump into motherhood clueless and continue to live in a state of adolescence for years far beyond their 20s and well into their 30s. So, our children are stuck with immature mothers. It's like the blind leading the blind. Taking a turn, shifting into a new gear so that we can care for the ones that need us the most will begin with the self-support. Explore the depths of your soul for what's there waiting for you to discover. Your life is waiting for you to catch up with itself. People always want to know what deja vu is. Well, my take on it is that you catch up with your life from the past, only to learn and then we slow down again because we disconnect with our higher self. The lessons are not always right away, but the lessons do come. We have tried for years to run from ourselves, but we are still there with all our old patterns and habits. The time has come for you to release and love yourself on a higher mental plane. You can support your friends, co-workers, lovers, and family, but what about you? Self-support will turn your life around. Meditate, pray, and build up the deep core of yourself so that the wisdom of the ancestors can shine upon you as they carry you through all situations. Settle into yourself with love and support, and watch your life grow.

SPEND TIME ALONE IN OBJECTIVE THOUGHT AS YOU CONSIDER THE DIRECTION OF YOUR LIFE.—I CHING

(The Receptive)

CHAPTER 9

Projecting the Best of Me Outward

We do things at times with the best intentions in mind, but things sometimes fall apart. Our lives are not pre-determined like you have always been told. Society has again programmed us into believing that we have no control of ourselves. You attract everything in your life with thoughts. Life really is what you make it. If you strive to do your best, then that's when you'll get the best that life has to offer. If you start failing mentally before you start the task, then it will be what you thought it would be— a failure. You can be down and out for only so long and at some point you will have to look up. Our intentions are only as good as we are. If you begin to look backwards like we all do, we can see how we could have, should have, and would have done things differently. What are you doing now in your life? How long are you going to swim with the sharks? We give our all on projects at work, for the kids' sports teams, and babysitting the neighbor's children and pets, all with good intentions. Are we feeling rewarded or fulfilled? Most of us are not. It's a duty to do these things, similar to washing our hands. Your mission should be to create goodness in your intentions, so that the growth of your soul can rise up and lift you to heights that can't be measured by the human mind. As you grow and move in a positive direction, there are going to be people who want to bring negative thoughts, situations, and distractions that will keep you off track. They are not going to understand that change is happening and their time is coming to an end. If you are meditating and praying continuously it will help you to keep the "haters" away. Additionally, it is important to remember why you are making the changes in the first place, whether you are moving out of an old relationship, starting a new job, adjusting to a new baby, or just plain tired of where you are, and know that a change must happen in order for you to find peace. The old patterns, habits and intentions will eventually go away. The way you used to think and feel is now a thing of the past. You are opening new doors, taking the shackles off, and breathing new life into yourself and your family, with an intense focus of staying on track so that you will be meeting the gifts that are for you right where you need to meet them in the now. Who are you to keep the past here in the future like smelly trash? Would you carry around dirty, smelly, rotten underwear? Let's hope not. If so, you're going to lose a lot of good people because of that smelly past. It's just like the old insecurities, patterns and habits that have also caused you to lose good people in your life; they can only take the smell for so long. People who come into your life and are trying to reach another level, or trying to fly on another plane will recognize the smell immediately. That's why we meet men and women that we really like and we don't see them or hear from them after a couple of dates. They have more than likely smelled the past, and let's hope that an old pattern wasn't to sleep with them right away, or else they're gone for sure. No one wants a smelly past in their bed with all of these needs right away. The intention is good but the timing is bad, because you have taken out your garbage from the past. What we think we are ready for, we are not. We can't change overnight. It can take years to really get to know yourself and others may get lessons right away. Your needs will change from day to day and year to year, but how you prepare and share them is the key. Time can be on your side if you use it right, and not waste it away on negative people, jobs, relationships, and things that tell us who we are before we can get to know us for ourselves. People will assume they know you because of the house you live in, the car that you drive or the way you dress. Life is more than the external things.

What really matters is the person that you have grown to be in the now. Once others see the glow all around you like a beaming light, their approach will be different, their conversation will be different and the respect for you will be different, because it takes a powerful person to re-create themselves into the real person that God wants them to be. People have been used to others thinking for them and doing for them, so to be around a free-thinker is a wonder. Build your life on everything good, create in goodness, love good, laugh good and grow worthy of yourself so that you can do unlimited things in harmony with nature the way it was intended.

"THE WORDS THEMSELVES, WHOLE, HOLY AND HEAL ALL MEAN THE SAME THING. TO HEAL IS TO REMEMBER WHO YOU REALLY ARE: A CHILD OF THE UNIVERSE, DIVINE AND LOVING AND INHERENTLY WHOLE".—LOUISE DIAMOND

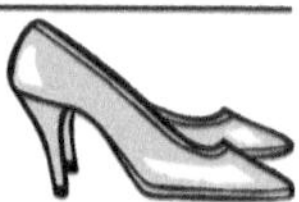

CHAPTER 10

Oh! We Love the Kids

There are days when we wake up and ask where has time gone? The kids have grown up and gone off to college, but they still are very much in need of our direction, even more now because they have adult problems just like us. Their rent is due, phone bill, insurance, not to mention school work, and the opposite sex has gotten their full attention. We remember the times when we would say things like, "Boy I'll be glad when you are older so that you can see what life is really like." It wasn't until my children had grown into young adults that I realized how much I depend on my mother for guidance and direction, even still to this day. Children are truly a blessing because it allows you to understand that God still loves the world enough to allow humans to arrive on earth. Stop to think what the world would be like if no one else could have children. The misdirection and miseducation of our children with all of our hang ups, opinions, religions, insecurities, anger and a list of other things can keep them from reaching their full potential. An environment has been created where we have lost sight of who we are. Within the African American community where

I grew up, most of us were raised in fatherless homes, and didn't meet our fathers until we were adults. By then, the relationship was out of touch. In some cases, mothers waited 14 to 15 years later to tell you who your father was because she was embarrassed about how the child was conceived in the first place. So from the conception, the child has deep rooted basics of shame or an unwanted feeling of embarrassment. We are parents, parents with values and morals that have been twisted into a frightening world wind of lies, secrets, and untold stories about who we really are and who our children are. How do you expect a child to recover completely from the wickedness that has been placed upon him or her? If we don't want to tell the children who their fathers are, we are certainly not going to share their Black history with them. We never take the time to simply ask the child if they are OK or what's wrong. We bring men into our children's lives, never asking their opinion about their feelings on this new stranger. We just feel that if a man is in the house it's enough. A man and a woman do not always complete a home, especially if one is positive and the other is negative or toxic. Women most times take on the task of trying to turn a negative into a positive. Just because a man is in the home does not make that a functioning home.

It's very hard to turn a negative voltage into a positive one. When we don't have our fathers we see anything as a family. It looks just like the image on television. MAN + WOMAN = FAMILY. That's what society has taught us—another misconception of real life, especially in the African American community. When we begin having children at a young age, we are not clear about what love really is, or have never been offered the notion that we must love ourselves first. The babies will flow out of a false sense of love, even with both parents in the home. When this happens we pay little attention to what our children's needs really are, and so the cycle will continue. As long as our community continues to relate in this way, there will be a disconnect with fathers, mothers and children. It's a part of the Post Traumatic Slave Syndrome. The things that have happened to African Americans here in America haven't happened by accident; it was designed that way. Families were not supposed to exist in our community; we weren't even looked at as human. So to try and bring all of these disconnected people together is a task at hand, and all the marching, fighting, and singing isn't going to help. Sure we have come a long way since slavery, but I think that we have come too far. We don't want to remember the horrible holocaust that occurred amongst our people. We can't heal our families, community, or ourselves if we forget. No other culture is asked to forget what has happened to their people except for African Americans. Our children are the future and so out of touch with who they are, and some will never be reached. Others will want to forget and become another race. We are a unique people here in America. We have fought every war, marched every march, played every game, worked in every job and fed people who hated our guts, for the survival of the next generation so that they can see a better tomorrow. We need to relate to our children on a different level. When I was growing up, the television signed off at midnight. Now, these children have cartoons 24 hours a day and we let them watch it, along with more than 500 additional channels. The media has consumed our children for the next 5 to 6 generations. The electronic devices are a part of their hands and ours. We are texting, viewing, and talking more than ever into these devices and not spending any quality time relating with our families. Let's get it clear; we are letting this happen. It's easy to turn on the television and allow it to babysit our children, teach our children, and show our children how to behave and love. Our job entails more than just working at these big corporate companies that could care less if we see our family or not. Years ago families worked next to each other. Now no one is together; only when the corporations tell us when to take off. Large companies are making more and more items to make it easier to parent so that these companies can get more work from you and you will see your family less and less. They're all one in the same; one hand washes the other. Now is the time to relate to your children. We are the ones they need the most for nurturing, supporting, directing and protecting. We have allowed the mass media to come into our homes in the form of food companies, clothing companies, shoe companies, and much more, not excluding the worst joke on us all—REALITY TV. It is time to get very clear about who runs your home and how it will be ran. Turn the television OFF; don't make it a Blockbuster night or a game night. Make it a real family night and talk about what you expect from your children and how you want them to live in the future. Give them hope about a better tomorrow through your experiences of life. Tell them the truth sometimes, and they just might start sharing the truth with you. Tell them to become creative and innovative about building our community, studying the stars, sun, moon and the people who were here before them that paved the way. If you don't know, ask or read until you find out, and please don't forget Mr. Google. What you see in yourself is what you will see in your children. This is why you see some families like the Jackson family that became successful, because that's what Joe Jackson saw within himself. If you see failure in you, you will nurse that down into your children. Pick up your life and your children will pick up theirs. Your children will follow you until you leave this earth, whether you are positive, negative or toxic. We now have two and three generations of men and women in prison because of these patterns. If you need help, go get it. Even if you don't think that you need it, go anyway. One session with a coach could never hurt. Make it your business to create harmony and relate with yourself, family and community. It all begins with YOU. Now what are YOU going to do?

"MY RELATIONSHIPS ARE A TRUE REFLECTION OF ME; I SURRENDER MY CHILDREN TO THE DIVINE FORCE THAT MOVES IN THROUGH AND FOR THEM; TODAY I WILL DO MORE THAN LISTEN, I WILL HEAR MY CHILDREN."

—IYANLA VANZANT

CHAPTER 11

Let the Sun Shine In Your Life

When you begin to change everything around you and within, you will feel different. Your eyes and ears are the first things that you will notice have changed. Your eyes are seeing things in a new way. You know that you are looking at the same things that you've always had, but now things are brighter, richer, vibrate in movement. Your ears are aware, alert, and the pitch has sharpened because change has arrived. Most of us have been walking around with our eyes wide shut and our hands over our ears. There are things that we didn't want to see before because of pain, insecurity, anger, and lack of confidence. With new vision comes great responsibility. People want to avoid responsibility, because it takes work and no one wants to work. Change means looking at life directly in the eye and moving through it as it comes day by day. Change means walking away from negative, toxic, and hurtful situations that have kept us in a frozen psychological state of mind. We all have a goal that we want to accomplish, but we sit for years waiting for the goal to achieve itself. We blame our children, our jobs, our partners, our parents, and never look at ourselves. The time for change is NOW. The only person holding you back at this point is you. No matter what your situation, the path has been laid for you to achieve greatness by the ancestors that came before you. If you had to take the voyage that they took, you wouldn't last a day at sea. The strength that brought you to the point of reading this book will take you to the next phase of your life. You know that you need a new life, job, car, partner, house and more money. Do you think that those things are going to knock on the door? NO! We refuse to release old patterns, but I'm going to tell you how to do it. Believe you can and take a step toward it by making a list of things that you want. Make a phone call, write a letter, and refuse to give up on your goal. Do something every day that will bring you closer to achieving it. Get focused and de-clutter your space, file your papers away. Answer unwanted mail with an explanation of how you will deal with the person trying to reach you. Whether it's a bill collector or an ex-lover, deal with it. Hiding from yourself and pushing away the people who are supporting you will only cause you more hurt and pain. The people who want to cause you pain and confusion will be put in their place as soon as you put them there. Meditate in peace with visions of what you want and need.

Shower your mind with visions that you have never even thought about before, like the big house with the pool overlooking the ocean, the kids secure and in the best schools, you starting your own business and it becoming a success. If you can see it, you can have it. If you can't see past your block, that is where you will always stay. Dream outside of the state or country that you live in; go around the world. The negative thoughts won't have time to enter in your mind and the people who once told you that it couldn't be done will be long gone, and if it was family members they're going to think that you are acting so funny they won't come around, which is GOOD. Your path will be clear. Once you believe and have a tremendous amount of faith, it will take you places that you've only dreamed about. When change happens deep down in the core of your soul, you will become such a powerful person that not just anyone can be within your presence. Have you ever been in the company of a great scholar or an entertainer? Their presence can't be contained in that one space. That's why people with this power are always traveling and moving only to be still to listen for more instructions. That's the part that we don't see about these powerful souls, they are moving to be still. Stillness keeps you clear and prepared. The powerful ones are studying, preparing, meditating and praying on another level because they understand what it takes for them to progress upward. Progress changes slowly and mindfully with awareness that will keep you in tune with yourself and the people, or things that you need to attract to you for your future. Become accountable for yourself so that growth will become a natural truthfulness daily. Your life will begin to unfold with exactness. The universe knows when to place people, jobs, and situations in your life that will propel you. Forget the past; it's dead, gone, history and will never return, but only if you keep your current mindset. The mind changes first and everything else will follow. Human beings are the only beings that pay for the same mistakes over and over; the rest of the animal kingdom keeps moving forward. They can't even conceive the notice of a mistake. Forward is the only way they know. As time passes and wounds have healed with love, you will know that your course is clear. This is your life, and this life is not a dress rehearsal. You can't do it over again, so live it to the fullest in joy, peace and inner harmony.

*"ACCEPT RESPONSIBILITY FOR YOUR LIFE.
KNOW THAT IT IS YOU WHO WILL GET YOU
WHERE YOU WANT TO GO, NO ONE ELSE."*

—LES BROWN

Daily Steps Forward Movement

CHAPTER 12

I Made It Through the Storm

When I first started this book it didn't even have a name. I just entitled it "the book". One day it just made sense to me to share my spirit and journey with the world, allowing openness and letting humility go. It may sound strange, but it made a lot of sense to me. When you know that your greatness is about to burst, the world in which you are in will begin to simply change. I realized that my dreams were being built before my very eyes and all I needed to do was **TAKE THE FIRST STEP**. I knew I needed to RELEASE! Release it all to the universe, to mother earth, to the great kings and queens that once ruled the motherland. Release for all the wrong that I had done, because those wrongs made me ALRIGHT. I know because I'm HERE! Here to make tomorrow a better day, for just my presence on earth proves that. There are those who will never know you were here on earth, but then there will be those who will miss your mere presence in a room when you are gone. I say be thankful for both. Balance your life with stillness and movement, no matter what you are going through. You have got to create peace for yourself;

no one is going to give it to you. You've got to take it and demand it from some people and situations. Be still in times where you need to listen and be obedient to the universe for further instructions. Keep moving forward with a positive outlook, aware of the steps that you must take to accomplish your goals. For instance, when you're with people and they say things like, "I'm just a moody person," those people choose to remain in that state of mind. Some for attention, but mostly because of low self-esteem. Those kind of people can and will become co-dependent upon you like any drugs, as something to hide behind. It runs deeper because usually it's the people closest to us, such as family, loved ones and friends. If you have someone that you are protecting by saying, "well that's just the way he or she is", because that's the way they are doesn't make those actions or their bad attitude (about everything) right. When growing up without knowing what tomorrow might bring, you begin to value time differently. Each moment in time that you are here to witness a day gone by, I say be thankful for it. Be thankful that you have a mind to move you out of your current situation. Look back on yourself only to reflect the old habits and patterns, but remember you can look back and you don't have to stay there to grow.

There are going to be things that will stick to your heart and tug at it for years. It's your heart and your emotions, go get it back mentally and re-energize yourself with the power that you are going to build you by ***TAKING THE FIRST STEP***. The first step releases the old habits, mentally going to the next level of your new insight which you are witnessing with yourself. You feel good about your future and high on life. You understand one thing now—your *living value*. You can put your feet in mother earth's soil, stand next to rocks and watch the ocean splashing. You can stand in moments of time and feel like you have touched yourself with a new understanding of life. We can recover memories to sharpen our future; it keeps us on track with real life. The past is forever gone, never to regain a moment of its time. If the now feels good, you are moving and in balance with your life. If the past patterns are holding you hostage, change it by surrounding yourself with good people, where you can truly feel their energy and spirit. Whatever and whoever you need in your life will be there. Feel good in every way and hold yourself accountable for taking you where you want to go. Eighty percent of the things that we worry about don't even manifest. We talk a lot about having faith, but at our true core we don't believe it and that's where the worrying comes in. You can be stressed, moody, angry, and your life will manifest these very things that you try to avoid. You have made it to the point where you can stand strong and now step back and see your true self. Believe in the things that your heart tells you. Show the future that you care by bringing your awareness full circle. Begin by listening, meditating, praying and reading. Listen to your heart, meditate on the earth for love and openness, and pray for truth about yourself as you see that it should be. Study yourself, as well as others. It will take a tight team of people to build your life, but allowing the right ones in will be based off of your needs at the time. People think I'm crazy sometimes when I tell them that I have outgrown my mother. I never said that she wasn't smarter, wiser, or smoother, but there comes a time when we must go out on our own and build our own homes and grow our own experiences. What are you going to tell your children? Everything your mother told you? Did she get it all right? Do you have any thoughts on the matter? Children can't always relate on a mother's level; that's an entirely different generation living in a whole new world. As parents we will get there one day too, but for now build your own life. Craft, shape, and take it in the direction that you want it to go. You can't live, borrow and rely on your mother forever. A mother's intent is to release us someday, but we become co-dependent on her for all of our needs, even her advice on a partner, what to eat, and how to cook it, and with lots of us, our mothers have tried or succeeded in passing down very negative and toxic patterns. For some, our parents have become co-dependent on us. The children that were kept so close, as soon as that child got a little air to breathe on their own, they tripped and fell into life and will not come back to the same because you were so busy protecting them, that you forgot to prepare them for life. What happens when you have an emotional, angry, confused, tired, selfish mother or father who will pass those toxic habits and patterns on to you? The cycle will continue. When your daughter or son comes to you about sex, be honest with them about life. The first man or woman that you sleep with may just be an experience, but don't take that first time of a sexual encounter and try to make it become the last. Most of us are not with the first guy or girl we ever slept with, and looking back some of us are glad that we're not. You see how some of those firsties turned out. Allow realness to come into those conversations so that she or he will know that life is real. Study things for yourself so that you will not run on someone else's knowledge and facts. It will take you to new heights. Gain the knowledge needed so that you will not arrive at the same place, which means that you have missed a lesson and you are back to learn it, but this time in a new way, for the new lesson that must come forward. Life will not stop for you to get the lesson, but it will catch you on the next go-round. If you learn stillness you can get the lesson the first time. Most of us move from house to house, man to man, school to school, and some have baby after baby. Society has us moving to the wrong vibration, and therefore our movements are off along with everything else in our lives. Move when the time is right; you will know and feel it. Time has a way of moving quickly, so prepare and study for readiness. Stay ready to make a change in a matter of moments, be a positive being, moving in moments of time that will change you, and watch the world continue to transform before your eyes.

"WE ALL NEED LOVE, SUPPORT, NURTURING, PASSION AND REAL RAW RELATIONSHIPS TO SURVIVE THE MANY TRIALS THAT WE WILL FACE, BUT WHEN YOU'RE ALONE GO INSIDE YOURSELF TO UNDERSTAND THAT YOU ARE THE REASON THAT YOU ARE HERE RIGHT NOW IN TIME. LIFE IS BEGINNING ANEW WITH EACH MOMENT THAT YOU ARE HERE. SEIZE IT NOW!"

—ANITA OSUIGWE-SPENCER

I started writing this book on the day that I was born. I went into labor on the 31st of June 2012 and gave birth to it on July 16, 2012. It was a labor of love; my way out of the old and going forward the best way I know how.

—Anita Osuigwe-Spencer

P.S. Thank you Patrick L.

Thank you so much Liltera R. Williams. You are the best! Let's write some more books...

www.ingramcontent.com/pod-product-compliance
Lightning Source LLC
Chambersburg PA
CBHW031403060726

47590CB00007B/2916